Polluted Oceans

by Ellen Lawrence

Consultants:

Suzanne Pleydell
PROJECT AWARE:
Protecting Our Ocean Planet—One Dive at a Time
Bristol, United Kingdom

Kimberly Brenneman, PhD
National Institute for Early Education Research, Rutgers University,
New Brunswick, New Jersey

Credits

Cover, © Colin Marshall/FLPA, © Richard Whitcombe/Shutterstock, © Africa Studio/Shutterstock, and © Flip Nicklin/Minden Pictures/FLPA; 2–3, © Luis Carlos Torres/Shutterstock and © Nikola Billic/Shutterstock; 4–5, © Biosphoto/Superstock; 5, © Rich Carey/Shutterstock and © Virunja/Shutterstock; 6–7, © Shutterstock; 8, © Ambient Images Inc./Superstock; 9, © Greenpeace/Alex Hofford; 10, © Kristina Vackova/Shutterstock; 11, © Bodo Marks/Corbis; 12, © aragami12345s/Shutterstock; 13, © Paul Hobson/FLPA; 14, © Richard Costin/FLPA; 15, © Rebecca Hosking/FLPA; 15B, © David Sischo/iStock/Thinkstock; 16, © age fotostock/Superstock; 17, © nui7711/Shutterstock; 18, © Jeff Greenberg/Alamy; 19, © Alexis Rosenfield/Science Photo Library; 20, © Jerome Wilson/Alamy; 21, © Tatiana Volgutova/Shutterstock, © Stephen McSweeny/Shutterstock, © Ruby Tuesday Books, © Kalmatsuy Tatyana/Shutterstock, and © auremar/Shutterstock; 22, © Shutterstock; 23, © Tory Kallman/Shutterstock, © sunsetman/Shutterstock, and © Jeff Greenberg/Alamy.

Publisher: Kenn Goin
Editor: Jessica Rudolph
Creative Director: Spencer Brinker
Design: Emma Randall
Photo Researcher: Ruby Tuesday Books Ltd

Library of Congress Cataloging-in-Publication Data

Lawrence, Ellen, 1967–
  Polluted oceans / by Ellen Lawrence.
     pages cm. — (Green world, clean world)
  Includes bibliographical references and index.
  ISBN 978-1-62724-236-3 (library binding) — ISBN 1-62724-236-8 (library binding)
 1. Marine pollution—Juvenile literature. 2. Marine ecology—Juvenile literature. I. Lawrence, Ellen, 1967– II. Title.
  GC1090.L39 2014
  363.739'4—dc23

2013041904

For more information, write to Bearport Publishing Company, Inc., 45 West 21st Street, Suite 3B, New York, New York 10010. Printed in the United States of America.

10 9 8 7 6 5 4 3 2 1

Contents

Dangerous Trash

In a warm, blue ocean, a sea turtle spots something white floating in the water.

It looks like a tasty jellyfish— but it's not!

It's a plastic bag drifting in the sea.

If the turtle eats it, the animal could get very sick and die!

- Every year, billions of pieces of trash end up in the ocean. The garbage includes plastic bags, bottles, soda cans, and even old tires!

How do you think garbage gets into the ocean?

plastic bag

sea turtle

Can you tell which is a plastic bag and which are jellyfish?
(The answer is on page 24.)

Dumped into the Ocean

Every day, huge amounts of trash get into the ocean. How?

Sometimes, people on boats dump their garbage into the ocean.

Other times, trash dropped on a beach is carried into the water by ocean waves.

Garbage dumped in a river can also be carried out to sea.

That's because all rivers eventually flow into the sea.

Look carefully at this picture. What are the different ways that trash can end up in the ocean?
(The answers are on page 24.)

People who work on fishing boats sometimes dump old ropes and torn fishing nets into the ocean.

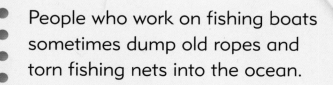

A Plastic Bag's Journey to the Ocean

1 A person drops a plastic bag on the ground instead of putting it into a trash can.

2 The wind blows the bag into a stream.

3 The stream flows into a large river, carrying the bag along.

4 The river flows into the sea. Now the plastic bag has reached the ocean.

7

Giant Garbage Patches

In parts of the ocean, floating trash gathers into huge areas called garbage patches.

One garbage patch in the Pacific Ocean is twice the size of Texas!

Most of the floating trash is made of plastic.

That's because plastic doesn't **decompose,** or rot away.

The plastic in a garbage patch may be in the ocean forever.

tiny pieces of plastic from the Pacific Ocean garbage patch

Over several years, plastic trash breaks down into tiny pieces. Some pieces are so tiny that they can't be seen.

This trash, which includes bottles, nets, and golf balls, was collected from the Pacific Ocean garbage patch.

Polluting Chemicals

Garbage is one kind of **pollution** in oceans.

Another kind is **chemicals,** such as those found in paint, glue, and **detergents**.

Sometimes, people on boats dump chemicals into the ocean.

Factories may also dump chemicals into rivers.

Then rivers carry the chemicals out to sea.

fish

a plastic bottle in the ocean

- Plastic is made from chemicals. As plastic trash in the ocean breaks down into tiny pieces, these chemicals get mixed into the water.

Why Is Pollution a Problem?

Pollution is very dangerous to animals that live in the ocean.

When ocean animals swallow seawater that has harmful chemicals in it, they may become sick or die.

Some animals get tangled in plastic bags or old fishing nets and ropes.

Then the animals can't swim to catch their food and they starve.

a fish killed by harmful chemicals

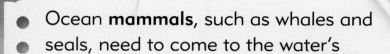

Ocean **mammals**, such as whales and seals, need to come to the water's surface to breathe air. Sometimes, these animals get trapped underwater in old nets and ropes. When this happens, they can't breathe and they drown.

seal

fishing net

Deadly Plastic Trash

Ocean trash is also dangerous to animals that mistake it for food.

Dolphins, fish, seabirds, and other animals sometimes eat plastic trash.

The animals can't **digest** the garbage and their stomachs get blocked.

As a result, the animals can't digest their normal food and they die.

plastic trash

a seabird called a puffin

Sometimes, seabirds feed plastic trash to their chicks by accident. When this happens, the chicks may die.

Scientists found this plastic trash in the stomachs of dead albatross chicks. Albatrosses are large seabirds.

albatross and chick

Oil Spills

Oil is another type of pollution that is very harmful to oceans.

If a ship that's carrying oil has an accident, oil can leak from the damaged ship.

The sticky, black liquid spreads through the water and may even wash up onto beaches.

When an oil spill happens, it can mean disaster for plants and animals.

a puffin covered in oil

- Ocean animals that swallow oil can get sick or die. Animals may also die of hunger because the fish or plants they usually eat have been killed by the oil.

workers cleaning a
beach covered in oil

Save the Ocean!

There's a lot that people can do to protect the world's oceans.

Factories must not dump trash or chemicals in rivers and oceans.

People on boats should take their trash back to land instead of throwing it into the sea.

People can also help out by cleaning up seashores.

Teams of **volunteers** pick up trash on beaches so it doesn't end up in the ocean.

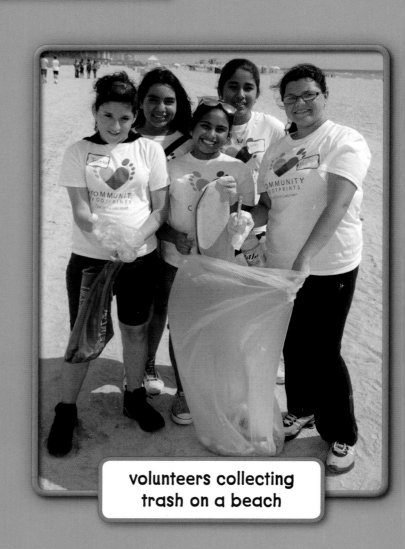

volunteers collecting trash on a beach

scuba diver

bag of trash

Some scuba divers pick up garbage on the bottom of the sea. Then the divers take the trash back to land, where it can be thrown away or **recycled**.

What Can You Do?

There's plenty that you can do to help keep oceans clean, too.

If you visit a river or beach, throw all of your trash in the garbage or recycle it.

Never leave trash outside because it can be blown into a river by the wind.

Then your trash could be carried out to sea.

By being careful with your trash, you'll be protecting oceans for the future!

- Never pour chemicals, such as paint, down **storm drains**. Chemicals in storm drains flow through underground pipes into rivers. The chemicals may then be carried out to the ocean.

20

Ways to Make Less Plastic Trash

Plastic can be harmful to animals if it ends up in the ocean.
Everyone can help make less plastic trash.

Reduce

When you buy a drink, reduce plastic trash by not using a straw.

Use cloth bags to carry groceries and other shopping items. This will reduce the amount of plastic bags that end up in the trash.

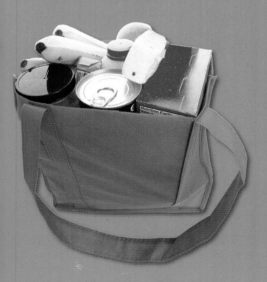

Reuse

Write a list of ways that you could reuse this clean, empty plastic yogurt container. For example, it could be used as a pencil holder or a pot for a plant. How many other uses can you think of?

Don't buy drinks in plastic bottles. Carry a drink in a bottle that you can reuse.

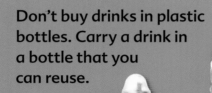

Recycle

Plastic trash, such as bottles and jars, can be recycled. Put plastic items into a recycling bin. The trash will be taken to a special factory. Here, the old plastic will be turned into new plastic items, such as more bottles.

Ocean Trash Collage

Turn trash into art by making a collage of the ocean. Here's how!

1. Think about what you would like your picture to show, such as sea animals living in a polluted ocean or a beautiful, clean ocean.

2. Glue clean trash to a large sheet of paper to create your collage. You can also include drawings.

3. Show your picture to your friends, family, or a teacher. Explain why people must never throw trash into rivers or the ocean.

4. Let everyone know how they can make less trash and recycle garbage. Be sure to point out that your picture is made from recycled trash!

You will need:

- Construction paper
- Paint, colored pencils, or markers
- Pieces of clean trash, such as plastic bottle caps or paper
- Scissors
- Glue

Give your picture a title.

The Polluted Ocean

Science Words

chemicals (KEM-uh-kuhlz) natural or human-made substances that can sometimes be harmful to living things

decompose (*dee*-kuhm-POHZ) to rot or break down into another form

detergents (dih-TUR-juhnts) substances made from chemicals that are mixed with water and used for washing dishes, laundry, and other materials

digest (dye-JEST) to break down food in the stomach and other organs so it can be used to give the body energy

mammals (MAM-uhlz) warm-blooded animals that have backbones, have hair or fur on their bodies, and drink their mothers' milk as babies; some mammals, such as dolphins, live in the ocean

pollution (puh-LOO-shuhn) materials, such as trash and chemicals, that can damage the air, water, or soil

recycled (ree-SYE-kuhld) when used, old, and unwanted objects are turned into something new and useful

storm drains (STORM DRAYNZ) holes in the ground, usually covered with metal grills; rainwater runs into a drain and flows through underground pipes until it empties into a river, a lake, or an ocean

volunteers (*vol*-uhn-TIHRZ) people who do work without pay to help others

23

Index

Read More

Jakubiak, David J. *What Can We Do About Oil Spills and Ocean Pollution? (Protecting Our Planet).* New York: PowerKids Press (2012).

Mason, Paul. *Oceans Under Threat (World In Peril).* Chicago: Heinemann (2009).

About the Author

Ellen Lawrence lives in the United Kingdom. Her favorite books to write are those about nature and animals. In fact, the first book Ellen bought for herself, when she was six years old, was the story of a gorilla named Patty Cake that was born in New York's Central Park Zoo.

Learn More Online

To learn more about ocean pollution, visit www.bearportpublishing.com/GreenWorldCleanWorld

Answers

Answer for page 5

This is a plastic bag.

Answers for pages 6–7

Ways that trash can end up in the ocean:

- People drop trash into rivers. Then it is carried out to sea by the rivers.

- Trash left on the ground is blown into rivers by the wind and carried out to sea.

- People drop or dump trash on beaches and it is washed out to sea.

- People drop trash into the ocean from boats.